AMPHIBIANS

Sarah Wilkes

WORLD ALMANAC® LIBRARY

Please visit our web site at: www.worldalmanaclibrary.com
For a free color catalog describing World Almanac® Library's list of high-quality books
and multimedia programs, call 1-800-848-2928 (USA) or 1-800-387-3178 (Canada).
World Almanac® Library's fax: (414) 332-3567.

Library of Congress Cataloging-in-Publication Data

Wilkes, Sarah, 1964-
   Amphibians / by Sarah Wilkes.
      p. cm. — (World Almanac Library of the animal kingdom)
   Includes bibliographical references and index.
   ISBN 0-8368-6208-2 (lib. bdg.)
   1. Amphibians—Juvenile literature. I. Title.
QL644.2.W59   2006
597.8—dc22   2005052624

This North American edition first published in 2006 by
World Almanac® Library
A Member of the WRC Media Family of Companies
330 West Olive Street, Suite 100
Milwaukee, WI 53212 USA

This U.S. edition © 2006 by World Almanac® Library. Original edition copyright
© 2006 by Hodder Wayland. First published in 2006 by Hodder Wayland, an imprint
of Hodder Children's Books, a division of Hodder Headline Limited, 338 Euston Road,
London NW1 3BH, U.K.

Subject Consultant: Jane Mainwaring, Natural History Museum
Editor: Polly Goodman
Designer: Tim Mayer
Illustrator: Jackie Harland
Picture research: Morgan Interactive Ltd and Victoria Coombs
World Almanac® Library art direction: Tammy West
World Almanac® Library editor: Carol Ryback
World Almanac® Library cover design: Jenni Gaylord

Photo credits: (t) top; b (bottom); l (left); right (r).
Cover photograph: a red-eyed tree frog.
Title page (clockwise from top left): Madagascan *Mantella*; European toad; red-eyed tree frog;
male and female Alpine newts. Chapter collage (from top to bottom): macro photographs of skin
of a horned frog, common frog spawn, the skin of a broad-mouth frog, a golden poison arrow frog
and a European toad.
CORBIS: / Joe McDonald cover. Ecoscene: / Clive Druett 4; / Paul Franklin 14(b); / Reinhard
Dirscheri 16; / Robert Pickett 28, 29, 30; / Anthony Cooper 35; / Wayne Lawler 42.
naturepl.com: / Morley Read 6; / Hans Christoph Kappel 8, 21; / Barry Mansell 9, 10, 20, 23, 26;
/ Doug Wechsler 11, 13; / John Cancalosi 12; / Fabio Liverani 14(t), 15, 31; / Pete Oxford 17, 24,
25, 27, 38, 41; / Mark Payne-Gill 18; / Marcelo Rocha/John Downer Productions 19; / David
Welling 22; / Ingo Arndt 32; / Phil Savoie 33; / Bruce Davidson 34; / Tony Phelps 36; / David
Shale 37; / Tim MacMillan/John Downer Productions 39; / Claudio Velasquez 40; / George
McCarthy 43. NHPA: / Daniel Heuclin 7.

Printed in China

1 2 3 4 5 6 7 8 9 10 09 08 07 06

CONTENTS

It is not possible to include information about every amphibian species in this book.
A taxonomic chart for amphibians appears on page 44.

WHAT ARE AMPHIBIANS?

Amphibians are animals that spend part of their lives in water and part of it on land. *Amphibian* comes from the Greek word *amphibios,* meaning "double life." The more than fifty-four hundred species of amphibians include frogs, toads, newts, salamanders, and caecilians.

Amphibians are a class of vertebrates. All vertebrates have a vertebral column, which is a series of small bones that run down their back to provide support. There are seven other classes of vertebrates, including mammals, birds, and reptiles.

Amphibian features

All amphibians share certain identifying features. They breathe through their moist skin as well as through their lungs. They have a long and often sticky tongue, and ears marked by eardrums, but they lack external ear flaps like mammals. Many species smell using an area of nerve endings in the roof of their mouth, called the Jacobson's organ. Most amphibians have four limbs, with four digits on the front limbs and five digits on the hind limbs. All amphibians are ectothermic, or cold-blooded. They must rely on heat from their environment to keep their body warm. Their body temperature fluctuates with the temperature of their surroundings.

The common frog (*Rana temporaria*) is a typical amphibian. It has moist skin and four limbs.

CLASSIFICATION

Biologists have identified several million unique organisms. They group together those with shared characteristics. The classification system moves through general to specific categories until each organism receives an exact binomial classification: a "last" name—the genus—and a "first" name—the species. The animal kingdom is divided into phyla (singular: phylum). Each phylum is divided into classes (also super- and subclasses), which are divided into orders (also super- and suborders) and then into families, genera (singular: genus), and species. A genus and species names a single organism that differs from all other organisms. In most cases, only members of the same species can reproduce with each other to produce fertile offspring.

The classification of the marbled salamander (*Ambystoma opacum*) is shown on the right.

KINGDOM: Animal

PHYLUM: Chordata

CLASS: Amphibia

ORDER: Caudata

FAMILY: Ambystomatidae

GENUS: *Ambystoma*

SPECIES: *opacum* (marbled salamander)

Use the first letter of each word in this sentence to remember the classification order:
Kings **P**lay **C**hess **O**n **F**ridays, **G**enerally **S**peaking.

Life cycle

All amphibians go through a series of physical changes called metamorphosis. Most species lay eggs that hatch into larvae. The larvae go through a number of physical changes to become adults. Frogs lay eggs that hatch into larvae, called tadpoles, that live in water and slowly change into small frogs. Most amphibians return to water to breed.

Amphibians are divided into three orders: caecilians (Gymnophiona); tailed amphibians (Caudata); and frogs and toads (Anura). This book looks at the orders and the families within them, and examines their characteristics and the way each group has adapted to its environment. Although it is not possible to cover all the amphibian families in this book, a complete taxonomic chart appears on page 44.

FROG LIFE CYCLE

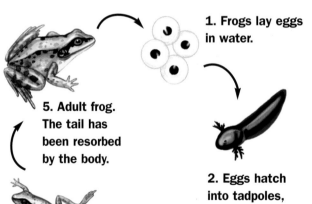

1. Frogs lay eggs in water.

2. Eggs hatch into tadpoles, which breathe using gills.

3. Tadpoles grow hind legs at 8 weeks and front legs at 12 weeks.

4. Froglet. The almost mature frog still has some of its tail but breathes through its lungs.

5. Adult frog. The tail has been resorbed by the body.

CAECILIANS (GYMNOPHIONA)

Caecilians are unusual, wormlike amphibians that look nothing like frogs or toads. They are found in tropical parts of South America, Africa, and Southeast Asia.

Shared features
The 176 species of caecilians are divided into six families. They range in size from about 3 to 60 inches (8 to 150 centimeters). All caecilians have a long body and no legs. Their tail is either tiny or virtually nonexistent. Their skeleton lacks pectoral (shoulders) and pelvic (hips) girdles. They have a massive skull but tiny eyes. Caecilians' external appearance is segmented, like a worm. Usually, their skin is moist and smooth—although a few caecilians have scales. Most caecilians have a single lung, but one species, *Typhlonectes eiselti*, has no lungs. This species obtains all the oxygen it needs through its skin and mouth.

Underground living
Caecilians spend much of their life underground. They use their heavy head to push through the soil in search of worms, insects, and other food, and to make burrows. They move forward using muscular contractions and by pressing against the ground.

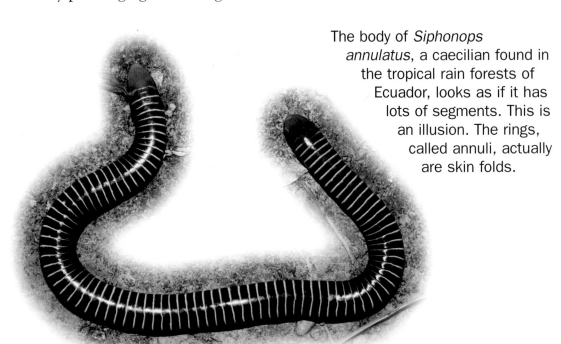

The body of *Siphonops annulatus*, a caecilian found in the tropical rain forests of Ecuador, looks as if it has lots of segments. This is an illusion. The rings, called annuli, actually are skin folds.

Caecilians have many needle-sharp teeth that they use to catch and hold their prey. This caecilian is eating a worm. Caecilians also prey on termites, beetles, mollusks, small snakes, frogs, and lizards. They swallow their prey whole.

Caecilians use a sensitive tentacle near their mouth to help find prey. The tentacle is retractable and is pulled in while burrowing. Caecilians hunt their prey by creeping up on it. They have two rows of small, sharp teeth on their upper jaw, and either one or two rows of teeth on the lower jaw that they use for gripping and crushing prey. Some caecilians produce a toxic secretion from their skin to defend themselves from predators.

Life cycle

All caecilians reproduce by internal fertilization. The male clasps the female in his teeth and deposits his sperm inside her. The fertilized eggs develop in one of three ways. In some species, the eggs are laid in burrows near streams and hatch into larvae with gills. The larvae wiggle into the water and undergo metamorphosis, gradually changing into adult caecilians that will live on land. In some egg-laying species, the larvae go through metamorphosis while still in the egg and break out as miniature adults. Often, these eggs are guarded by the female. The third type of life cycle involves live bearers—species that give birth to live offspring. The eggs stay inside the female's body for nine to eleven months, hatching into larvae inside her. The larvae feed on a milklike secretion produced by the female before they emerge as tiny adults.

KEY CHARACTERISTICS
GYMNOPHIONA
- **Long body; no limbs; virtually no tail.**
- **Heavy skull and small eyes.**
- **Segmented appearance.**

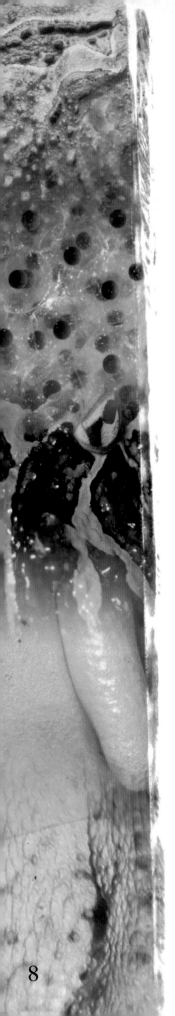

TAILED AMPHIBIANS (CAUDATA)

Tailed amphibians make up the second-largest amphibian order. The order Caudata contains 470 species of sirens, salamanders, and newts found all over the world except in Australia and Antarctica.

The order Caudata is divided into three superfamilies: sirens (Sirenoidea); giant salamanders (Cryptobranchoidea); and salamanders and newts (Salamandroidea). The different superfamilies are identified by the position of various bones in their skull. The adults range in size from a few inches (cm) to just under 6.5 feet (2 meters).

Caudata features

Tailed amphibians are easily distinguished from other amphibians because the larvae, juveniles, and adults all have a tail. The tail is particularly long in the adults. Most adults, except for the siren, have two pairs of legs of similar size that extend at right angles from their body. The siren lacks hind limbs. The larvae have teeth on both their upper and lower jaw, as well as gill slits and external gills.

The European fire salamander (*Salamandra salamandra*) is a relatively large salamander, ranging in size from 5 to 12 inches (12 to 30 cm). A double line of poison glands runs along its back. Other poison glands line both sides of its body.

Reproduction

Sirens and giant salamanders are ancient amphibians that fertilize their eggs in the water. This is called external fertilization. After the female releases the eggs, the male fertilizes the sperm in the water. Salamanders and newts use internal fertilization.

KEY CHARACTERISTICS
CAUDATA

- Tail present in larvae and adults.
- Two pairs of legs of similar size, except in sirens.
- Larvae have gills, external gill slits, and teeth on upper and lower jaws.

Habitat

Some tailed amphibians are terrestrial, living most of their life on land, while others are aquatic and spend their entire lives in water. Some terrestrial amphibians return to water to breed, but some lay their eggs on land. Most terrestrial species live on the forest floor. They hide under rocks or logs in the daytime and emerge at night to feed. Aquatic species live on the bottoms of streams or ponds, often under stones.

Food

Tailed amphibians are carnivorous animals that hunt a range of invertebrates, including worms and insects. They often use their long tongue to catch prey. Their well-developed tail provides power when swimming.

The Alabama waterdog (*Necturus alabamensis*) is a medium-sized salamander that measures 6 to 9 inches (15 to 22 cm). It has well-developed legs and four digits on both front and back feet. The adults retain their external gills and have fins.

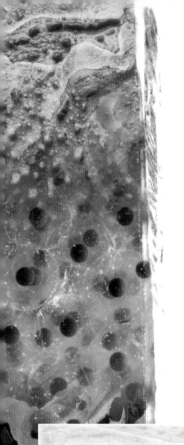

SIRENS (SIRENOIDEA)

Sirens are eel-like salamanders that live in water. The four species of sirens are native to the southeastern United States and northeastern Mexico.

Siren features

Sirens range in length from a few inches (cm) to just under 3 feet (1 m). They have a streamlined body that moves easily through water, small forelimbs, and no hind limbs. They have eyes but no eyelids. Sirens do not have teeth at the front of their mouth. Instead, they have a horny beak. The adults are unusual because they have large, external gills and gill slits.

KEY CHARACTERISTICS
SIRENOIDEA

- **No hind limbs and reduced forelimbs.**
- **Large, external gills.**
- **Horny beak instead of teeth at the front of the mouth.**

Habitat

Typically, sirens live in ditches, swamps, and lakes with slow-moving water and lots of vegetation. They are active predators that hunt aquatic invertebrates. They pull their prey into their mouth using suction created by expanding the size of their throat. Sirens also eat aquatic plants.

Surviving droughts

Sirens can survive prolonged periods of drought by burrowing into the mud at the bottom of ponds. They wrap their body in a protective cocoon formed from layers of skin cells, leaving their mouth uncovered so they can still breathe. They may remain cocooned in the mud for several months, waiting for rain.

Sirens, such as this Rio Grande lesser siren (*Siren intermedia texana*), have external gills and an elongated, finned tail to aid swimming.

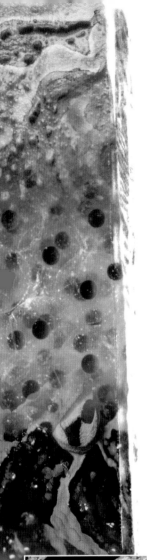

GIANT AND ASIATIC SALAMANDERS (CRYPTOBRANCHOIDEA)

The superfamily Cryptobranchoidea consists of two families: giant salamanders (Cryptobranchidae); and Asiatic salamanders (Hynobiidae). Giant and Asiatic salamanders are large, tailed amphibians.

Giant salamanders

Giant salamanders have a massive head and body and a relatively short tail. They do not have eyelids. There are three species: the Chinese and Japanese giant salamanders and the North American hellbender. All three species are aquatic, but unlike sirens, they do not use gills to breathe. Instead, a large fold of skin along the sides of their body increases the surface area for oxygen absorption. They use lungs to breathe.

Asiatic salamanders

Asiatic salamanders are considered the most ancient of the tailed amphibians. Some are terrestrial, while others live in fast-moving water. All species breed in streams. Their bodies are slender with a long tail. They have eyelids. Their lungs are either small or completely absent, so they breathe through their skin.

The Pacific giant salamander's (*Dicamptodon ensatus*) smooth, brownish-gray skin with black blotches camouflages it well against riverbeds. It makes a "barking" sound when frightened.

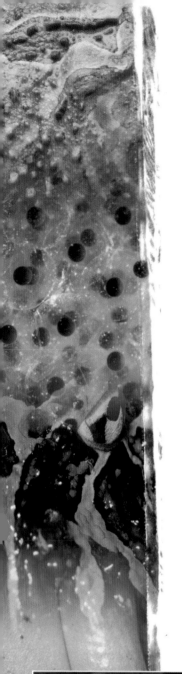

NEWTS AND SALAMANDERS (SALAMANDROIDEA)

Newts and salamanders are a superfamily of tailed amphibians. They are distinguished from the other superfamilies in the order by internal fertilization.

It is easy to confuse a member of this superfamily with a small lizard because they all have long tails. The amphibians, however, can be identified by the number of digits on their forelimbs: newts and salamanders have only four digits, while lizards have five. The term *salamander* is generally used to describe a tailed amphibian that lives mostly on land, while a newt returns to water to breed.

Classification

The superfamily Salamandroidea contains about fifty-four species divided into seven families: Pacific mole salamanders; mole salamanders; newts and European salamanders; olms, mudpuppies, and waterdogs; torrent salamanders; Congo eels; and lungless salamanders. The amphibians in each family are quite varied in their appearance, and no one feature is present in all families except for internal fertilization.

Mole salamanders are named after the fact that they spend much of their life in burrows. Olms, mudpuppies, and waterdogs are aquatic amphibians with feathery gills and lungs. Olms live in caves. They are blind and lack any skin pigment. Lungless salamanders form the largest family. They do not have

Great crested newts (*Triturus cristatus*) return to water to breed. They have dark, gray-brown backs and sides covered with darker-colored spots that provide good camouflage in the ponds where they breed.

lungs and absorb oxygen only through their skin and mouth. This limits their activity and makes them inactive for long periods of time. Lungless salamanders must live in damp habitats so that their skin does not dry out. They are nocturnal (active at night).

Newts and European salamanders are a diverse family. Salamanders tend to have smooth skin, while the skin of newts is rough. Most species have well-developed lungs. Members of the newts and European salamanders family are brightly colored and generally small, rarely exceeding 8 inches (20 cm) in length. They all produce toxins in their skin. The most poisonous salamanders and newts, such as the American red-spotted newt, have bright warning colors used in defensive displays. Most newts spend several months in the water during the breeding season. European salamanders live in burrows or under logs and stones in damp woodlands and subalpine meadows, emerging only on mild, damp nights.

KEY CHARACTERISTICS
SALAMANDROIDEA

- **Presence of a tail.**
- **Internal fertilization.**

The lungless Northern red salamander (*Pseudotriton ruber*) lives in the eastern United States. It prefers woods and meadows close to clear, cool water.

Life cycles

Newts and salamanders follow one of three different life cycles: amphibious, terrestrial, or aquatic.

Amphibious life cycle

Most newts and salamanders undergo an amphibious life cycle. The eggs hatch as aquatic larvae with external gills and transform into terrestrial adults that breathe using lungs and/or their skin. In spring, the adults return to water to breed. The adults spend several months in the water. Their bodies change slightly to adapt to this habitat. Their skin becomes more permeable to oxygen, their tail becomes more flattened to aid swimming, and their eyes change shape in order to focus in water. They also develop a line of sense organs running from behind the head to the tail that detect vibrations in the water. Some males and females become more brightly colored and carry out a courtship display.

The tail on this newt embryo is barely visible as it develops inside its egg, which was laid on the leaf of an aquatic plant. The newt larva develops within the egg and hatches after two to three weeks.

Female newts and salamanders lay their eggs individually on leaves. The eggs hatch into larvae that are similar in appearance to the tadpole larvae of frogs. The front legs appear first, soon followed by the back legs. The external gills disappear and are replaced by lungs. Once the lungs form, the larvae go to the surface of the water to breathe. After this stage, the rest of the body develops. When the eyes, digestive system, and organs mature, the salamanders or young newts are ready to leave the water.

Newt larvae take about four months to metamorphose into adults. This is the larva of a great crested newt (*Triturus cristatus*).

Alpine newts (*Triturus alpestris*) develop bright breeding colors. The male (left) has blue markings and a prominent crest along its back. The female (right) has a mostly black body with an orange underside.

Terrestrial life cycle

A few species, such as the red-backed salamander, do not have an aquatic stage in their life cycle. Their eggs are laid under logs and develop directly into adults. The entire larval stage takes place within the egg, and miniature adults emerge from the eggs.

NEWT LIFE CYCLE

Female great crested newts lay two or three eggs a day between March and mid-July, until two to three hundred eggs have been laid. They lay the eggs on submerged aquatic plants, each one carefully wrapped in a leaf. The larvae hatch after about three weeks and metamorphose into juveniles about four months later.

Aquatic life cycle

Some species, such as the axolotl, have an aquatic life cycle, in which the amphibian does not appear to metamorphose at all and keeps a larval appearance throughout its life. The axolotl spends its entire life underwater, except for occasional trips to the surface to gulp a breath of air. Adult axolotls look just like large tadpoles with three pairs of bushy gills at the back of their head. Axolotls undergo an internal metamorphosis: The changes taking place inside its body are hidden from view.

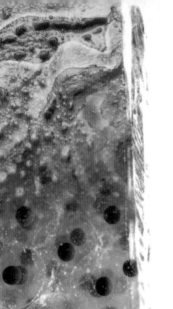

FROGS AND TOADS (ANURA)

The order Anura is the largest and most diverse of the amphibian orders. Frogs and toads are found all around the world except in the Arctic and Antarctica—although most species live in the world's tropical regions.

The extra-long hind legs of this European toad (*Bufo bufo*) help propel it through water. The webbed toes aid swimming.

KEY CHARACTERISTICS
ANURA

• **Long back legs with elongated ankles.**
• **Short backbone.**
• **Most species lack ribs.**
• **Large, bulbous eyes.**
• **Wide mouth.**

Anura features

There are about 4,750 species in this order, divided into twenty-eight families. All frogs and toads have a body adapted to jumping. Their back legs are particularly long because their anklebones are enlarged to make an extra section in their leg. Their backbone is short and rigid to withstand the force of landing. Nearly all frogs and toads lack ribs, which is another adaptation to leaping. The force of landing would break their ribs.

Adult anurans, with a few exceptions, do not have a tail, although the tadpoles have a long tail that slowly disappears as they go through metamorphosis. Their eyes are large and bulbous, and their mouth is wide. Virtually all frogs and toads have a long tongue to catch prey. Their eardrums are located behind their eyes. They breathe using their lungs and through their moist skin.

Anurans have one of two basic body shapes, with the shape being an adaptation to their habitat. One group of anurans, such as European frogs, has a slender body with long back legs and a long head with a tapering snout. These frogs and toads tend to live in water. If they venture onto land, they stay near water so they can jump back in when startled. Their streamlined bodies help them swim and jump more easily. The second group includes those frogs and toads that live on land or burrow in the ground. They have squat bodies, shorter legs, and feet with stubby digits that are suitable for digging.

The order Anura is divided two large suborders, known as Archaeobatrachia and Neobatrachia. Archaeobatrachians are featured on pages 20 to 23, and the Neobatrachians are covered on pages 24 to 41.

FROG OR TOAD?

There are no real differences between frogs and toads. Some species may be called frogs in some parts of the world and toads in others. Many people consider the drier, warty skin to be characteristic of the toad, but that is not always the case.

Tree frogs have adapted to living in trees. Their large digits help them grip. This South American species, *Hyla lindae*, lives in the rain forests of western Ecuador.

This African bullfrog male (*Pyxicephalus adspersus*) instinctively works to rescue tadpoles stranded in a shrinking pool of water. The adult frog digs a channel to more water.

Habitats

Most frogs and toads that live in temperate regions of the world are not active during the winter months. Since they are ectothermic, they rely on heat from their environment to keep their bodies warm. In the cold winter months, they enter a deep sleep called torpor. While in torpor, they do not use energy to stay warm, so they survive without eating. Those species that live in very cold environments have a natural antifreeze in their bodies to prevent ice from forming in their body cells.

At the other extreme, desert frogs and toads face a different set of problems. During the dry season, when their pools dry up, these frogs survive by estivating—they dig themselves into mud until the rains start again. Their bodies dehydrate, or lose water, to the mud. When the rains return, they rehydrate, or resorb, water from the mud. Some desert-living species have water-storage organs inside their bodies that keep them alive during estivation. When it rains, temporary pools form, and the frogs immediately emerge from the mud, mate, and lay their eggs. Their tadpoles must complete their metamorphosis in the short time that the water remains in the pools. Once the water dries up, any tadpoles that have not matured into adult frogs die.

Food and hunting

Frogs and toads are predators. They hunt a range of small prey animals, such as worms, slugs, snails, beetles, flies, and spiders. They catch smaller prey by flicking out their long, sticky tongue and grip larger prey with their jaws and their backward-facing teeth.

Camouflage and warning colors

Frogs and toads are also preyed upon by many animals. They avoid predators in a variety of ways. Some rely on camouflage, such as a skin color that blends in with their surroundings. Poisonous species rely on their bright coloration to warn predators that they are poisonous.

The false-eyed frog from South America (*Physalaemus biligonigerus*) fools predators with the two large eyespots on its back.

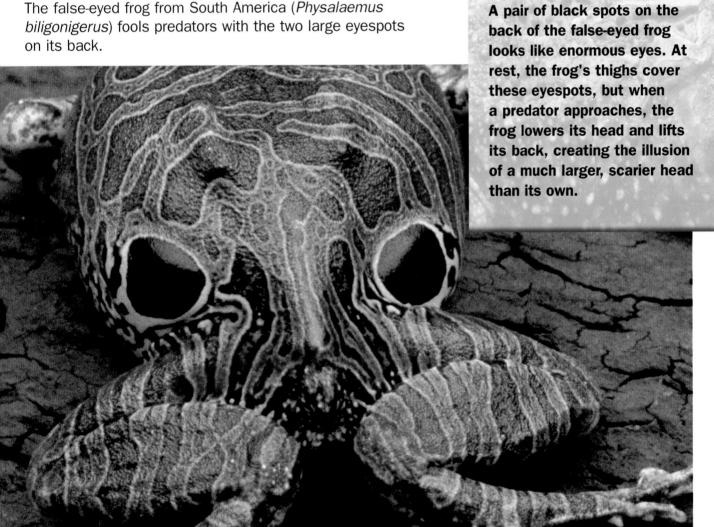

FALSE EYES

A pair of black spots on the back of the false-eyed frog looks like enormous eyes. At rest, the frog's thighs cover these eyespots, but when a predator approaches, the frog lowers its head and lifts its back, creating the illusion of a much larger, scarier head than its own.

ARCHAEOBATRACHIANS (ARCHAEOBATRACHIA)

The tiny tail of this tailed frog (*Ascaphus truei*) is just visible. Only the males have this tail. They use it to fertilize the eggs inside the female. Tailed frogs lack the eardrums that are present in other frogs.

The suborder Archaeobatrachia is made up of nine families of relatively ancient frogs and toads. There are about one hundred fifty species, some of which are found in just one or two places in the world. The frogs and toads in each family differ from each other internally and also in their method of reproduction.

Tailed frogs

Tailed frogs are the oldest family of frogs. They are unusual because the adults have a short tail. They also have free ribs (not attached to their breastbone) in their chest. Only two species of tailed frogs exist, and they live in the fast-flowing mountain streams of North America. These nocturnal frogs show a number of adaptations to fast-flowing water. The males have extra-large forearms to grip the female when mating so that she is not swept away. The eggs are laid in strings under rocks to protect them from the current. Living in a cold environment slows down their growth rate, so these frogs take several years to metamorphose. They do not breed until they are at least seven years old.

Fire-bellied toads

The most distinguishing feature of fire-bellied toads is their brightly colored undersides, which are orange or red with black spots. The bright colors warn predators that these toads are distasteful. When threatened, fire-bellied toads lift up their body to reveal their colored underside to frighten off predators.

Midwife toads

European midwife toads are small, squat toads with a rough skin. They are mostly terrestrial and mate on land. Females lay eggs in long strings that a male catches and wraps around his hind legs. The male carries the eggs around for several weeks. When they are ready to hatch, he takes them to a pool. By carrying the eggs with him, the male protects the eggs from predators and disease, increasing the chances that more tadpoles will hatch and live to adulthood.

The male midwife toad (*Alytes obstetricans*) carries yellow strands of eggs on his back for about thirty days. During this time, he cannot mate with other females. The females continue to produce eggs, which are carried around by other males.

Asian toadfrogs

Asian toadfrogs live near streams in Southeast Asia. Their tadpoles are also adapted for life in streams. They hang onto rocks with large, suckerlike mouths to keep being carried away by the current. Malaysian horned toads have hornlike growths above their eyes and on their nose. The body is mottled brown and green, providing perfect camouflage on the forest floor.

Spadefoot toads

Spadefoot toads live in the dry areas and deserts of Europe and Western Asia. They are nocturnal and come out only during cool nights to hunt insects and spiders. They shelter themselves in cool burrows in the daytime. In the hottest season, spadefoot toads retreat into deep burrows, where they stay for several

SPADEFOOT TOADS

Spadefoot toads have hard growths on their hind feet. These clawlike "spades" help them dig cool, underground burrows in their dry habitats. Unlike most burrowing animals, spadefoot toads dig with their hind feet in a backward spiral path, gradually disappearing into the earth.

Spadefoot toads, such as this plains spadefoot (*Scaphiopus bombifrons*), are named after the small, black "spade" on the first toe of each hind foot. This hardened pad allows them to dig into the loose soil without damaging their toes.

months. Although they lose a lot of water from their bodies, they are able to survive. Spadefoot toads breed after the rains arrive. Their tadpoles often metamorphose into young toads in just three weeks.

Clawed frogs and Surinam toads

These toads are fully aquatic and are adapted to living in water. Their bodies are flattened, and their legs stick out sideways—an arrangement that is good for swimming but hopeless for walking on land. Their webbed feet help them swim, and their eyes point upward so they can see animals moving in the water above them. Clawed frogs and Surinam toads are very unusual because they don't have tongues. They feed on small fish and the larvae of aquatic insects, which they catch and shovel into their wide mouth using their forelimbs.

Surinam toads have an unusual life cycle without a free-swimming larval stage. The life cycle starts when the male grips the female to mate. The female lays her eggs, which the male fertilizes and sweeps up with his feet. He places them on the female's back. The eggs stick to her back and become embedded in her skin. When the eggs hatch into tadpoles, they stay in a pocket in the female's skin. Several months later, tiny toadlets emerge and leave their mother.

The African clawed frog (*Xenopus laevis*) is an aquatic species that spends its life in water. Its front feet are not webbed. Its webbed back feet have sharp, black claws on the inner toes.

23

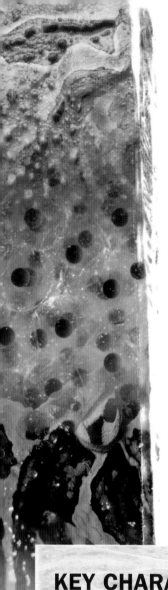

LEPTODACTYLIDS (LEPTODACTYLIDAE)

This is a large family of frogs found throughout Central and South America, the southern parts of North America, and on islands in the Caribbean Sea.

The family Leptodactylidae is part of the suborder Neobatrachia (*see page 44*). There are 864 species, including the false-eyed and the white-lipped frogs. Some are relatively large frogs, about 10 inches (25 cm) long, but the suborder also includes a few tiny species.

Shared features

All the frogs in this family have a particularly wide mouth and teeth on their upper jaw. Some species, such as the Brazilian horned frog, have a horned appearance because of hornlike flaps above their eyes.

KEY CHARACTERISTICS
LEPTODACTYLIDAE

- **Teeth on upper jaw.**
- **Wide mouth.**

The Amazon horned frog (*Ceratophrys cornuta*) has small horns above its eyes. It digs itself under leaf litter so that just its head sticks out as it waits for prey. It jumps out and swallows the prey in one swift snap of its mouth.

Subfamilies

Leptodactylidae is split into four subfamilies: Ceratophryinae; Hylodinae; Leptodactylinae; and Telmatobiinae. Ceratophryinae is a small group of large-headed, aggressive, carnivorous frogs. The Leptodactylinae are mostly terrestrial, but some live in trees where they build foam nests for their eggs. The adults secrete mucus from their skin and reproductive tracts, which they beat into a foam with their legs. The eggs are laid in the foam nest, which protects the eggs from drying up. In several frog species, one of the parents stays close to the nest to protect it.

The Lake Titicaca frog (*Telmatobius culeus*) of South America is the largest aquatic frog in the world. About thirty years ago, these frogs often grew to about (12 inches) 30 cm and weighed 2.2 pounds (1 kilogram). Today, Lake Titicaca frogs are much smaller because the larger frogs have been collected for food. Only the smaller frogs are left to breed in the wild.

Surviving in the Andes

Some frogs in the subfamily Telmatobiinae live in mountain lakes high in the Andes Mountains of Peru and Bolivia, at altitudes of 13,124 feet (4,000 m). These frogs have to cope with cold air and water, low oxygen levels, and high levels of ultraviolet radiation (the harmful rays in sunlight that can cause skin cancers in people). The extraordinary Lake Titicaca frog has adapted to survive in its low-oxygen environment. Its extra-baggy skin absorbs more oxygen, which allows the frog to stay submerged for long periods of time while avoiding exposure to ultraviolet radiation. Lake Titicaca frogs move their hind legs around to create small disturbances in the water and bring fresh oxygenated water closer to their bodies. Their blood is unique, too. It has the smallest red blood cells of any amphibian but the highest amount of a protein called hemoglobin. The hemoglobin in red blood cells carries oxygen around the body, so the more hemoglobin an animal has, the more oxygen it carries in its blood.

True Toads and Harlequin Frogs (Bufonidae)

True toads and harlequin frogs are found across North and South America, Africa, Europe, and Asia. Most species are terrestrial, although some live much of their lives in streams, and a few live in trees.

Shared features

There are about 376 species in the family Bufonidae, ranging in size from 1 to 100 inches (1 to 25 cm) in length. All species have a pair of poison glands that ooze a toxic, milky fluid to deter predators. The poison is stronger in some species than others, but even in its mildest form, the poison causes a burning sensation if it contacts the eyes or mouth of a predator. The secretion is particularly toxic in the brightly colored harlequin frogs, whose warning colors show that they are poisonous.

True toads

The term *true toads* refers to species that belong to the family Bufonidae. Most move by hopping and crawling rather than leaping. They have thick, warty skins, a stout, short body, and relatively short, thick legs.

Harlequin frogs

Harlequin frogs differ from most toads because they have a slender body and long legs. They lay their eggs in fast-flowing streams. Their tadpoles are adapted to this moving environment: Suckers on their abdomen grip the surface of rocks and stop them from being carried away.

The male harlequin frog (*Atelopus varius*) does not call. It attracts females using visual displays, such as leg and head twitching, stomping the ground, or hopping in one spot.

Breeding

True toads breed in ponds. Many species take part in mass migrations to their breeding ponds every year. In early spring, thousands of European toads cross roads to reach their breeding ponds. They follow the same route every year. Once they reach the ponds, the toads form pairs. The male grips the female as she lays eggs, and the eggs are fertilized externally. Most toads lay long chains of eggs in water, although a few species lay their eggs on leaves above the water.

Problem toads

Most toads are considered useful animals because they eat large numbers of insects and slugs that are pests in backyards and crops. In 1935, cane toads were introduced to Queensland, Australia, to control insect pests in sugarcane fields. The plan backfired. The introduced toads ate beneficial insects as well as pests, and soon the toads themselves became pests. Cane toads are now hunted in an attempt to stop them from invading new habitats, where they threaten the survival of native species.

KEY CHARACTERISTICS
BUFONIDAE

- Heavy skull and a mostly sturdy body with short legs, except for harlequin frogs.
- Skin secretes toxic substances.

The poisonous skin secretion of the cane toad (*Bufo marinus*) can sicken or kill animals that bite or try to eat it, including small mammals, such as dogs and cats, and snakes.

POISON FROGS (DENDROBATIDAE)

These small, brightly colored frogs are also called poison-arrow or poison-dart frogs. Some Native peoples in South America rub their blowgun darts over the backs of the species *Phyllobates terribilis* to smear them with poison. Not all frogs in this family are poisonous.

Shared features

There are about 170 different species of poison frogs, including the strawberry frog and the blue poison-dart frog. They are all small, ranging in size from 1 to 1.5 inches (2.54 to 4 cm). They have slender limbs and toes with adhesive pads for gripping.

Three species of Dendrobatidae are extremely dangerous. The deadliest of these brightly colored frogs is *Phyllobates terribilis*. The poison from one frog can kill twenty thousand mice or eight humans. This poison, called batrachotoxin, oozes out of pores in their skin. Interestingly, poison frogs are not as poisonous when kept in captivity. Scientists believe the frogs' natural diet of insects from the rain forest increases the potency of their poison.

The yellow and blue poison frog (*Dendrobates tinctorius*) is one of the larger poison frogs, measuring up to 2 inches (5 cm) long.

KEY CHARACTERISTIC
DENDROBATIDAE

- **Toxic skin secretions.**

28

Habitat

Poison frogs live in the tropical rain forests of Central and South America, where they come out by day and hop along the forest floor. In these forests, the air temperature and humidity stay much the same all year round. This is important to poison frogs because they require a humidity of at least 80 percent. If the humidity drops, these tiny frogs can dry up and die within a few hours. The temperature must stay around 72 °Fahrenheit (22 °Celsius). Some species live in cooler, humid forests on mountain slopes.

A chemical from the phantasmal frog (*Epipedobates tricolor*) is about two hundred times more effective than morphine in laboratory tests. Researchers hope to mimic its effects for use as pain-killing medications for humans.

Breeding

Female poison frogs lay a small clutch of three to five eggs on leaves on the ground. When the eggs hatch, the male usually carries the tadpoles on his back, one by one, to a stream or pool of water. Sometimes the male chooses a tiny pool of water trapped in the leaves of plants, such as bromeliads. The females of some poison frog species lay unfertilized eggs as food for their tadpoles. The males can be territorial, guarding an area of the forest floor. If another male intrudes, there may be a fight, with the males wrestling each other using their back legs. Strawberry poison frogs are very territorial, and a male will defend its territory to the death.

TREE FROGS (HYLIDAE)

Hylidae is a large family of frogs adapted to life in trees. They are found in North and South America, Europe, northern Africa, Southeast Asia, and Australia.

There are more than seven hundred species of tree frogs, including marsupial frogs, chorus frogs, and leaf frogs. Most tree frogs live in trees and can jump from branch to branch. Some species are aquatic, while others spend their lives on the ground. Most species are small frogs, less than 2 inches (5 cm) long, but a couple of species grow up to 5.5 inches (14 cm) long.

Shared features

Tree frogs have a slender, slightly flattened body with long, thin legs. They have horizontal pupils and webbed feet. The ends of their toes are enlarged to form adhesive pads that they use for gripping and climbing. Extra segments of cartilage between the last two bones of each toe allow their toes to swivel and keep flat against all surfaces. Some tree frogs have

The red-eyed tree frog (*Agalychnis callidryas*) has very obvious red eyes. During the day, the frog sleeps with its eyes closed so that its green body blends in better with its surroundings. If disturbed, it opens its huge red eyes to scare off any predators.

elaborate skull bones that form a kind of helmet, called a casque. Casque-headed frogs use their helmet to seal the entrances to their burrows, which reduces the amount of water lost by evaporation.

Breeding

Since tree frogs are arboreal (live in trees), most species lay their eggs on leaves in trees. Leaf frogs lay clusters of eggs on leaves above pools of water. The female frog keeps the eggs moist by urinating on them until they hatch. The tadpoles drop into pools below as they hatch. Other tree frogs lay their eggs in a protective nest of foam. The adult frogs whip up mucus into a foam with its back legs, into which the female lays her eggs. The foam hardens and protects the eggs. When the tadpoles hatch, they wiggle free of the nest and drop into the water below.

Marsupial frogs

Marsupial frogs carry their young in a pouch, just like marsupial mammals, such as kangaroos. The female Australian marsupial frog (*Assa darlingtoni*) deposits a few large eggs into moist soil. When they hatch, the male stands over them, and the tiny tadpoles wiggle into slitlike openings on his hips. These act as pouches in which the tadpoles are carried around. Only about half the tadpoles make it to the safety of the pouches. The male carries the tadpoles for forty-eight to sixty-nine days, until their metamorphosis is complete and young frogs emerge from the male's skin. In other species of marsupial frogs, the female carries the tadpoles.

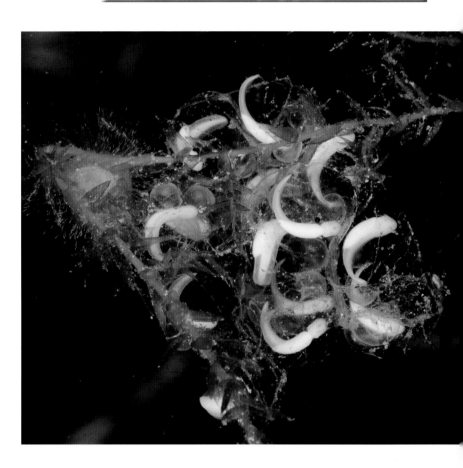

Common tree frog (*Hyla arborea*) eggs develop underwater. This frog lives among trees and bushes for much of the year but lays its eggs in shallow water. The female lays clusters of up to fifty eggs, with each egg measuring about 0.08 inches (2 mm) in diameter.

GLASS FROGS (CENTROLENIDAE)

Glass frogs are found in tropical parts of Central and South America. The greatest number of species occur in the rain forests of Costa Rica and Panama, and on the forested slopes of the Andes Mountains.

The family Centrolenidae contains one hundred four species, including the reticulated and emerald glass frogs. As more rain forests are explored, even more species of glass frogs are discovered.

Shared features

Glass frogs were named after their partly transparent skin. Their internal organs are visible. Their upper surface is usually green with yellow, white, blue, or red markings. Most species are smaller than 1 inch (2.54 cm) in length, although a few species grow to just under 3 inches (8 cm). They have a small, wide body and a blunt head. Their small eyes lie almost on the top of the head.

The bones and digestive system of this glass frog, (*Hyalinobatrachium* sp.), are just visible.

A male glass frog (*Centrolenella fleischmanni*) guards its eggs. Parental care ensures that more of the tadpoles will hatch than if the eggs are ignored.

KEY CHARACTERISTICS
CENTROLENIDAE

- **Partly transparent skin.**
- **Blunt head.**
- **Extra leg section with one bone instead of two.**

Glass frogs have horizontal pupils and, like many other tree-living frogs, enlarged toes for gripping. Glass frogs have an extra section in their leg, but unlike species in other families of the Anuran order, it contains just one bone instead of two.

Egg laying

Glass frogs live high in trees near mountain streams. Like many other types of tree frogs, they lay their eggs on leaves that overhang streams. Many species show parental care, with the male frogs guarding small clutches of eggs. When the eggs hatch, the tadpoles fall into the water below, where they live in the mud and leaf litter at the bottom of streams. This habitat is low in oxygen. The tadpoles' blood flows very close to the surface of their skin so it can pick up as much oxygen as possible. Since their skin is partly transparent, the color of the blood shows through the skin, giving the tadpoles a bright red appearance.

Male glass frogs are territorial. They defend a small area of the forest from other frogs of the same species. In particular, they guard the places from which they make their calls to attract females. The call of a glass frog is a high peep or whistle. In some species, the call of a single frog may imitate a chorus to attract more females.

TRUE FROGS (RANIDAE)

True frogs live in almost every habitat except for extremely cold areas. They are found all around the world, including islands in the Caribbean Sea.

Shared features

The family Ranidae contains 643 species, including the common frog, wood frog, goliath frog, and edible frog. Ranging in size from 1 to 12 inches (2.54 to 30 cm), true frogs are characterized by long, muscular hind limbs that usually end in webbed feet. Their long legs and webbed feet help the frogs swim. Their body has a slender, streamlined shape. The head is pointed, and their eyes are large and bulbous, with horizontal pupils. They have teeth on their upper jaws. Their skin is usually smooth, although a few have a slightly warty skin. The color of their skin is usually a combination of browns and greens that blends well with the ground and provides good camouflage.

Habitat

Most true frogs are terrestrial, living on land for much of the year. They move around by hopping and jumping. Some species can tolerate brackish water—water that is partly freshwater and partly saltwater. The crab-eating frog survives in salty mangrove swamps.

The African bullfrog (*Pyxicephalus adspersus*) has three large teeth sticking out from its lower jaw, which it uses to fight off predators and hold onto prey. This bullfrog is eating a mouse.

Life cycle

Most true frogs have an amphibious life cycle, spending time on land but returning to water to lay their eggs. A few species lay their eggs on land, and those eggs hatch directly into tiny adults.

Most species lay clumps of eggs, called frog spawn, in water. The eggs hatch into free-swimming tadpoles. Some frog species lay their eggs in flowing water. Their tadpoles have disks on their abdomen to grip stones on the riverbed so they do not wash away.

Some species of frogs, such as the European common frog, gather together in large numbers during the breeding season. The females lay their eggs in clumps beside those of other females. Scientists believe the clumps help the eggs survive cold weather. The thick layer of jelly in each egg acts as insulation, while the black embryo in the middle absorbs heat from the Sun. Together, these features mean that the temperature in a clump of eggs can be several degrees warmer than the surrounding water, which is just enough to stop them from freezing during a cold spring night.

Scientists once believed that as the male common frog (*Rana temporaria*) held the female as she laid her eggs, he fertilized all the eggs in the clutch. New research indicates that other males also release their sperm over the eggs after the first male frog leaves, so the eggs are often fertilized by more than one male.

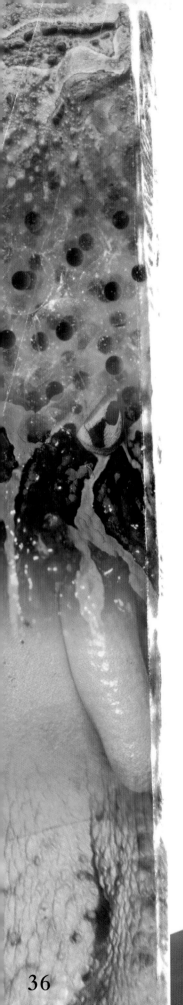

REED AND SEDGE FROGS (HYPEROLIIDAE)

Reed and sedge frogs live in Africa, Madagascar, and the Seychelles Islands. These arboreal frogs have bright, distinctive markings. Hyperoliidae contains 234 species, including bush frogs, marbled reed frogs, and sedge frogs.

Shared features

Reed and sedge frogs are relatively small frogs, measuring 1 to 3 inches (2.54 to 9 cm) long. They have moderately long legs and slender, streamlined bodies with no ribs. Their toes have enlarged disks for gripping, their eyes have horizontal pupils, and they have teeth on their upper jaws. Many species have smooth, brightly patterned, almost metallic-looking skin.

Reed and sedge frogs are nocturnal, emerging at night to feed on a variety of prey animals, such as insects, spiders, and slugs. Some species, such as the *Tornierella* sp., specialize in eating snails exclusively, while the spine reed frog (*Afrixalus fornasinii*) preys on the eggs of other species of frogs.

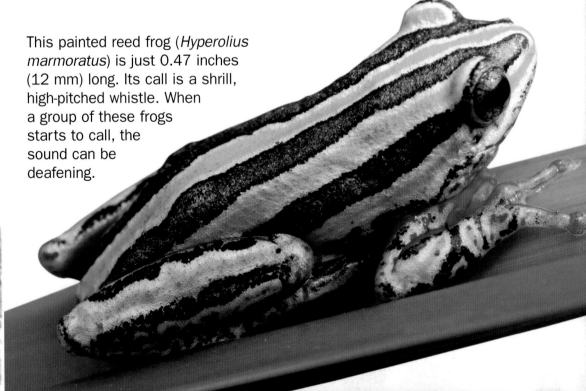

This painted reed frog (*Hyperolius marmoratus*) is just 0.47 inches (12 mm) long. Its call is a shrill, high-pitched whistle. When a group of these frogs starts to call, the sound can be deafening.

Egg layers

Reed and sedge frogs resemble tree frogs in many ways. For example, most live in trees and lay their eggs on branches that overhang water. Some sedge frogs lay their eggs in holes in trees. A few lay their eggs on the ground so that after they hatch, the tadpoles must crawl and wiggle their way over the ground to reach water.

Color change

Some reed and sedge frogs can change the color of their skin. In some species, the skin color varies with the temperature of the surroundings. Some species of reed frogs, including the spiny reed frog, which is found in dry habitats in Africa, range in color from almost white in the hot season to copper at cooler times of the year. The paler skin reflects the Sun's heat, which helps cool the frog and reduces water loss. The arum lily frog lives in wetlands in South Africa. These frogs are sometimes found in white arum lily flowers, where they change their skin color to white to match their surroundings. This makes them virtually invisible to predators as well as to their insect prey. When the flowers die, the frogs turn brown to match.

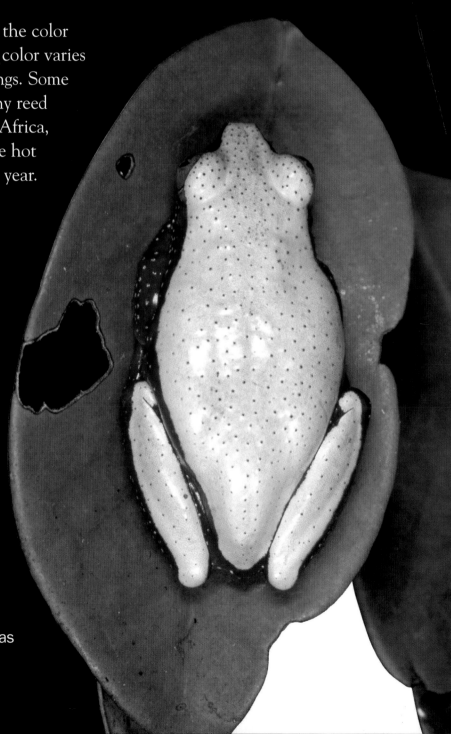

This spiny reed frog (*Afrixalus fornasinii*) has turned white in the sunlight. Its usual skin color is brown.

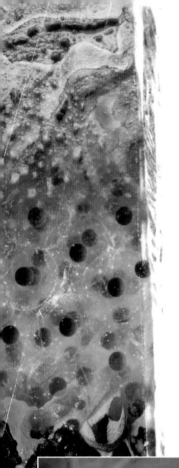

OLD WORLD TREE FROGS (RHACOPHORIDAE)

Old world tree frogs are found in tropical parts of Africa, Madagascar, and across Asia from India to Japan, including the islands of Southeast Asia.

This family contains about 276 species, including Wallace's flying frogs, Madagascan *Mantellas* sp., and gray tree frogs. Their sizes range from about0.6 inches (1.5 cm) to 5 inches (12 cm). Most of these frogs are arboreal, although there are a few terrestrial species.

Madagascan *Mantellas*, such as this golden Mantella (*Mantella aurantiac*), look very similar to the poison frogs of South America. These two families of frogs evolved separately from one another.

Shared features

Most old world tree frogs have webbed feet, and the webs are often brightly colored. In some species, the webs between the feet are enlarged to help the frog glide from tree to tree. Like all tree frogs, members of this family have enlarged disks on their toes for gripping branches. They have teeth on their upper jaws, and their pupils are horizontal.

Mantella frogs

The *Mantella* sp. frogs of Madagascar are similar to the poison frogs of South America, although they are not closely related. Like other poison frogs, *Mantella* sp. frogs secrete a toxin and are brightly colored. Their poison comes from the plants they eat and oozes from their skin. Mantella frogs are not as poisonous as poison frogs from the Western Hemisphere. If someone were to handle a *Mantella* sp. frog and then touch his or her mouth, the worst effect would be numb lips.

Mantella sp. frogs tend to live near bamboo plants. The males are violently territorial and will defend an area of up to 22 square feet (2 square meters) around a "well" of water, such as a rain-filled stalk of broken bamboo. When a female answers the call of a chirping male, the male leads her to his well. If she likes the well, the female lays one egg, which the male fertilizes. She then attaches the egg to the side of the well above the water level. The egg hatches in about ten days, and the tadpole drops into the water. The female visits the tadpole regularly to lay more unfertilized eggs for the tadpole to eat.

Flying frogs

Wallace's flying frogs have feet with extra-large webbing that acts as a parachute. These nocturnal gliding frogs can make sharp turns in midair. Gliding is an efficient way to move about. The frogs can descend quickly from the highest branches to breeding sites near the forest floor. They can also glide from tree to tree without reaching the forest floor, where they are at risk from predators.

KEY CHARACTERISTICS
RHACOPHORIDAE

- Broad, flat skull.
- Webbed feet.
- Enlarged disks on toes for gripping.
- Teeth on upper jaw.
- Horizontal pupils.

The Wallace's flying frog (*Rhacophorus nigropalmatus*) can glide for distances of up to 148 feet (45 m). Like most tree frogs, it has pads on its toes to help it grip when landing.

NARROW-MOUTHED FROGS (MICROHYLIDAE)

Narrow-mouthed frogs are found in tropical regions of the world, such as Central and South America, central and southern Africa, parts of India, and across Southeast Asia.

There are more than four hundred species in this large family, including the tomato frog, rain frog, and sheep frog. They range in size from just 0.4 inches (1 cm) to 4 inches (10 cm). Most species are nocturnal. Their habitat varies from wet, tropical rain forest to arid desert and savanna. Many of these frogs are arboreal, but some species are terrestrial. The terrestrial species spend the day sheltering in burrows and emerge at night to feed.

Shared features

Narrow-mouthed frogs have a small, pointed head with a narrow mouth, a rounded body, and short legs. They do not have teeth or webbed feet, and most have eyes with horizontal pupils.

Rain frogs, such as this Namaqua rain frog (*Breviceps namaquensis*), burrow into the ground during dry weather. They are named after the way they come to the surface after rain. The males then call to the females.

Breeding

Narrow-mouthed frogs lay their eggs either in water, in burrows, or in the tiny pools of water trapped inside the leaves of bromeliads. During mating, most males grip the female around her middle. An African species called breviceps is so round and short-legged that it is impossible for the male to grip the female. Instead, he secretes a sticky substance that glues him to the female. Breviceps frogs build a foam nest in which the female lays her eggs.

Tomato frogs (*Dyscophus* sp.) are terrestrial and live in forest habitats. Many forests on Madagascar have been cleared, but tomato frogs have adapted well to living in farmland and even in backyards.

Tomato frogs

Most species of narrow-mouthed frogs have a brown or gray body but a few, such as tomato frogs, are brightly colored. Tomato frogs are found on Madagascar. Their bright color acts as a warning. These frogs are not poisonous, but they can produce a sticky, white, skin-irritating mucus that deters predators. Tomato frogs can also discourage predators by inflating their bodies like a balloon.

KEY CHARACTERISTICS
MICROHYLIDAE
- **Small, pointed head.**
- **Rounded body.**
- **Relatively short legs.**

The frog and the spider

Some species of narrow-mouthed frogs living in South America have a strange relationship with theraphosid spiders, a type of tarantula. One such frog species is *Chiasmocleis ventrimaculata*. These frogs live in the burrows of theraphosid spiders, which is quite risky because the spiders normally prey on small frogs. For some reason, the spiders tolerate this particular species. The frogs share the spiders' burrows during the day and emerge at night to feed. In some cases, the frogs have been seen hiding under the spiders when threatened by a predator. The frogs benefit from the protection offered by the spiders, but researchers aren't sure how the spiders benefit.

UNDER THREAT

New species of amphibians are being discovered all the time, especially small species that live in rain forests. Hundreds of other species, however, are either becoming extinct or are under the threat of extinction.

Environmental damage
One of the main reasons for the global decline in amphibians is the loss of habitat. Rain forests are being cleared at an ever-increasing rate, and wetland habitats and ponds are disappearing, too.

Another major threat is global warming. One of the effects of global warming is climate change and extreme weather events such as droughts, storms, and flooding. Amphibians are very sensitive to changes in their surroundings and cannot tolerate changes in climate, however small.

Some ponds and streams are polluted by fertilizers and sewage that add nutrients to the water. This can lead to massive growths of algae, which disrupts the food chains of frogs and toads, forcing them to move away.

Acid rain affects amphibians, too. Acid rain is rain that contains pollutants, such as sulphur dioxide and nitrogen oxides, that make rainwater more acidic than normal. When acid rain falls on ponds, lakes, and rivers, it increases the acidity of the water and harms the eggs of amphibians.

Pesticides harm amphibians in different ways. Weed killers or insecticides are sometimes accidentally sprayed on amphibians. In some places, the discovery of frogs with deformed legs and strange pigmentation has been linked to the use of pesticides. When insects, slugs, and snails are killed by pesticides, amphibians lose their food source. They may also be poisoned by eating prey that has been sprayed by pesticides.

Disease

Disease is killing thousands of frogs around the world. In Britain, common frogs are dying from a disease called red leg. This is a fungal disease that spreads from pond to pond, killing all the frogs. Frogs are dying from similar fungal diseases in North and South America and Australia, too.

Conservation

One of the best ways to conserve amphibians is to protect existing habitats and create new ones. New amphibian habitats can be created by clearing waste from ponds and ditches and building new ponds in backyards and on farmland. A simple pile of logs can shelter amphibians for the winter.

Many toads are killed on roads every year during their annual migration to their breeding ponds. In some places where toads are known to cross every year, special tunnels under busy roads help toads cross safely. In other places, local people protect the toads by carrying them across the roads during the breeding season. For the rare frog species, however, the only way to ensure their survival is to breed them in captivity.

A toad tunnel built under this road allows toads to reach their breeding ponds safely. Many countries build tunnels under new roads to allow toads, frogs, and mammals such as badgers, to cross safely underneath.

BRED IN CAPTIVITY

Captive breeding rescued the Mallorcan midwife toad from the brink of extinction. Once considered extinct, a few of these toads were discovered in the mountains of Mallorca, Spain, in 1980. Twenty toads were moved to the Jersey Zoo in the Channel Islands and bred. In 1989, seventy-six toads were released back into the wild in Mallorca. Mallorcan midwife toads are now reclassified as "vulnerable" instead of "critically endangered."

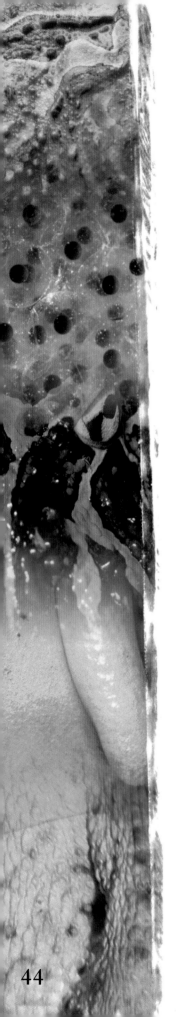

AMPHIBIAN CLASSIFICATION

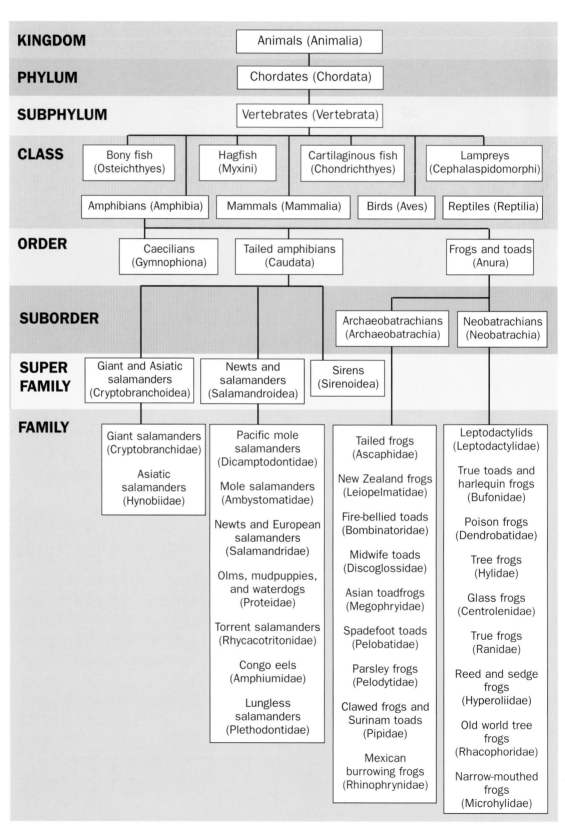

KINGDOM	Animals (Animalia)			
PHYLUM	Chordates (Chordata)			
SUBPHYLUM	Vertebrates (Vertebrata)			
CLASS	Bony fish (Osteichthyes)	Hagfish (Myxini)	Cartilaginous fish (Chondrichthyes)	Lampreys (Cephalaspidomorphi)
	Amphibians (Amphibia)	Mammals (Mammalia)	Birds (Aves)	Reptiles (Reptilia)
ORDER	Caecilians (Gymnophiona)	Tailed amphibians (Caudata)		Frogs and toads (Anura)
SUBORDER			Archaeobatrachians (Archaeobatrachia)	Neobatrachians (Neobatrachia)
SUPER FAMILY	Giant and Asiatic salamanders (Cryptobranchoidea)	Newts and salamanders (Salamandroidea)	Sirens (Sirenoidea)	
FAMILY	Giant salamanders (Cryptobranchidae)	Pacific mole salamanders (Dicamptodontidae)	Tailed frogs (Ascaphidae)	Leptodactylids (Leptodactylidae)
	Asiatic salamanders (Hynobiidae)	Mole salamanders (Ambystomatidae)	New Zealand frogs (Leiopelmatidae)	True toads and harlequin frogs (Bufonidae)
		Newts and European salamanders (Salamandridae)	Fire-bellied toads (Bombinatoridae)	Poison frogs (Dendrobatidae)
		Olms, mudpuppies, and waterdogs (Proteidae)	Midwife toads (Discoglossidae)	Tree frogs (Hylidae)
		Torrent salamanders (Rhyacotritonidae)	Asian toadfrogs (Megophryidae)	Glass frogs (Centrolenidae)
		Congo eels (Amphiumidae)	Spadefoot toads (Pelobatidae)	True frogs (Ranidae)
		Lungless salamanders (Plethodontidae)	Parsley frogs (Pelodytidae)	Reed and sedge frogs (Hyperoliidae)
			Clawed frogs and Surinam toads (Pipidae)	Old world tree frogs (Rhacophoridae)
			Mexican burrowing frogs (Rhinophrynidae)	Narrow-mouthed frogs (Microhylidae)

GLOSSARY

abdomen the part of the body of a vertebrate that lies between the thorax (chest) and the pelvic girdle (hips).

acid rain rain containing acid formed in the atmosphere from waste gases.

adaptation a change in order to suit the environmental conditions.

antifreeze a substance that prevents water from freezing.

aquatic living in water.

arboreal living in trees.

beneficial having a good effect.

breed to reproduce.

breeding season the time of year when animals mate and lay their eggs.

bromeliads plants that live on trees in rain forests.

bulbous rounded, swollen, and bulblike in shape.

camouflage colors and patterns that blend with the surroundings.

carnivorous meat-eating.

cartilage a tough, elastic connective tissue that forms part of the skeleton in vertebrates.

characteristic a feature of an animal; for example, having webbed feet or a wide mouth.

dehydrate to lose water.

digits fingers or toes.

ectothermic cold-blooded; having a body temperature that rises and falls with the surrounding temperature.

embryo an early stage of a vertebrate's life before birth.

estivating becoming dormant during a period of hot weather.

extinct no chance of ever existing or living anywhere again.

eyespots eyelike markings.

fertilization the fusing of an egg (from the female) and sperm (from the male) to form a zygote, a new individual.

fungal relating to or caused by a fungus. A fungus is a type of organism that feeds on organic matter.

gill a body part used by an aquatic animal to absorb oxygen from water.

gill slits narrow, external body openings through which water passes from the gills to the environment.

habitats the places where animals or plants live.

hemoglobin a blood protein containing iron that carries oxygen.

humidity moisture in the air.

insecticides chemicals used to kill insect pests.

invertebrates animals that do not have a backbone.

Jacobson's organ a sensory organ in the roof of an amphibian's mouth.

juveniles young, immature adults.

larva a young animal that looks different from the adult and changes shape as it grows.

metamorphosis the process of changing appearance; for example, a larval animal changing into an adult.

migration a regular journey between two different places at certain times of the year.

GLOSSARY (CONTINUED)

morphine a drug that can be used to kill pain

mucus a sticky substance consisting of water and protein.

nocturnal active at night.

oxygenated enriched or supplied with oxygen.

permeable able to allow liquids and gases to pass through.

pesticides chemicals used to kill pests such as insects, fungi, or weeds.

pigment a substance that produces a characteristic color in a plant or animal tissue.

predator an animal that catches and kills other animals.

prey an animal that is caught and killed by a predator.

rain forests dense forests with a high level of precipitation and a huge variety of plants and animals.

red blood cells blood cells that contain hemoglobin and carry oxygen around the body.

reticulated looking like a net; having a mesh pattern.

savanna a grassland habitat with few trees; found in tropical parts of Africa.

secrete to release a liquid substance, for example, poisons from the skin.

sp. an abbreviation for *species*, used as part of the Latin name for animals when the exact species is unknown.

sperm male gamete, or sex cell.

streamlined having a shape that moves easily through air and water.

subalpine the habitat on mountain slopes just below the treeline.

surface area the entire surface that forms the outside covering of an object, plant, or animal.

tadpole the larval stage in the life cycle of a frog or toad.

temperate a moderate climate that lacks extremes in temperature.

terrestrial living on land.

territory a range or area claimed and defended by an animal.

torpor a state of inactivity.

toxic harmful, poisonous.

tropical occurring in parts of the world just north and south of the equator; a hot, wet climate.

ultraviolet radiation (UV) short, harmful wavelengths that make up part of the invisible portion of sunlight. Most UV radiation is absorbed by Earth's atmosphere.

vertebrate an animal that has a backbone; for example, fish, amphibians, reptiles, and birds.

webbed feet having skin connecting the toes, which is helpful for swimming.

FURTHER INFORMATION

BOOKS

Clark, Barry. *Amphibian*. *Eyewitness Books* (series). Dorling Kindersley (2000).

DK Animal Encyclopedia. Dorling Kindersley (2000).

Forshaw, Gould, and McKay, eds. *The Encyclopedia of Animals: Mammals, Birds, Reptiles, Amphibians*. Fog City Press (2002).

Ganeri, Anita. *Animal Groupings*. *Nature Files* (series). Chelsea House (2004).

McKay, George, et al. *The Encyclopedia of Animals: A Complete Visual Guide*. University of California Press (2004).

Morgan, Sally. *Animal Kingdom: Amphibians*. Raintree (2004).

O'Shea, Mark, and Tim Halliday. *Reptiles and Amphibians*. *Smithsonian Handbooks* (series). Dorling Kindersley (2002).

Solway, Andrew. *Classifying Living Things: Classifying Amphibians*. Heinemann Library (2003).

Spilsbury, Louise. *Classification: From Mammals to Fungi*. *Science Answers* (series). Heinemann Library (2004).

Taylor, Barbara. *Visual Encyclopedia of Animals*. Dorling Kindersley (2000).

Wallace, Holly. *Classification*. *Life Processes* (series). Heinemann Library (2001).

WEB SITES

http://frogweb.nbii.gov/index.html
Discover the details behind the decline of amphibians in North America.

http://yahooligans.yahoo.com/content/animals/amphibians/amph_families.html
Get the facts on amphibian families.

www.enchantedlearning.com/coloring/amphibians.shtml
Explore the Enchanted Learning Web site on frogs and other amphibians.

www.nationalgeographic.com/kids/creature_feature/0203/frogs.html
Follow the links on this creature feature to learn about red tree frogs.

www.nwf.org/frogwatchUSA/
Learn what's going on with frog conservation in your state.

www.truthout.org/docs_04/printer_101604G.shtml
Find out why one-third of Earth's amphibians face extinction.

www.washingtonpost.com/wp-dyn/articles/A33569-2004Oct14.html
Read more about amphibians as indicator species.

INDEX

Page numbers in **bold** refer to a photograph or illustration.